Library Resources

What Would You Do with an
Atlas?

Susan Kralovansky

Consulting Editor, Diane Craig, M.A./Reading Specialist

A Division of ABDO
ABDO
Publishing Company

visit us at www.abdopublishing.com

Published by ABDO Publishing Company, a division of ABDO, P.O. Box 398166, Minneapolis, Minnesota 55439. Copyright © 2013 by Abdo Consulting Group, Inc. International copyrights reserved in all countries. No part of this book may be reproduced in any form without written permission from the publisher. Super SandCastle™ is a trademark and logo of ABDO Publishing Company.

Printed in the United States of America, North Mankato, Minnesota

102012
012013

 PRINTED ON RECYCLED PAPER

Editor: Liz Salzmann
Content Developer: Nancy Tuminelly
Cover and Interior Design and Production: Kelly Doudna, Mighty Media, Inc.
Photo Credits: Kelly Doudna, Shutterstock

Library of Congress Cataloging-in-Publication Data

Kralovansky, Susan.
What would you do with an atlas? / Susan Kralovansky.
p. cm. -- (Library resources)
ISBN 978-1-61783-606-0
1. Atlases--Juvenile literature. I. Title.
912--dc15

2012946824

Super SandCastle™ books are created by a team of professional educators, reading specialists, and content developers around five essential components—phonemic awareness, phonics, vocabulary, text comprehension, and fluency—to assist young readers as they develop reading skills and strategies and increase their general knowledge. All books are written, reviewed, and leveled for guided reading, early reading intervention, and Accelerated Reader® programs for use in shared, guided, and independent reading and writing activities to support a balanced approach to literacy instruction.

Contents

What would you do if you had an Atlas?

If you had an atlas, you could learn about the Earth!

5

An atlas is a collection of maps.

A map provides information about a place.

A globe is a world map in the shape of the Earth.

Some maps show the whole Earth.

Other maps show just part of it.

7

With an atlas you can find North America, Africa, or Australia.

Where is Australia?

Check out this atlas. It has a map of Australia.

An atlas shows you where places are.

Australia is south of Indonesia.

An atlas is a guide to the world. It shows where places are. It can also have more information about those places.

Many atlases have a few pages in the beginning that explain how to use the maps.

Wow! I want to learn about the world!

Using an atlas is fun! But there are some important things to know about atlases.

Almost every map has three things. The first is a legend. The legend tells you what the words and symbols on the map mean.

What kinds of symbols do maps have?

This map marks capital cities with stars. Other cities have small dots.

I learned this from the legend.

15

The bar scale converts miles and kilometers to inches and centimeters.

Now I know how far it is from Los Angeles to San Diego!

The abbreviation mi stands for miles. The abbreviation km stands for kilometers.

16

The second thing most maps have is a bar scale. The bar scale helps you measure distance on the map.

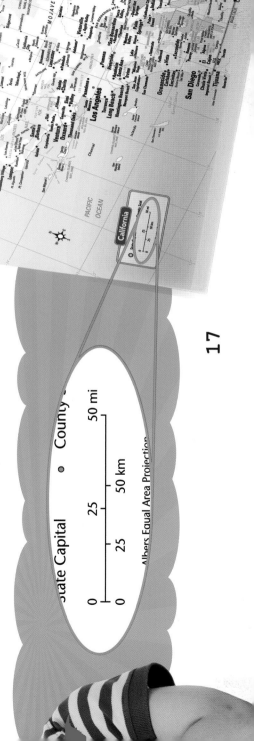

State Capital   •   County

0   25   50 mi

0   25   50 km

Albers Equal Area Projection

California

The third thing on a map is a compass rose. A compass rose shows the four directions on a map.

North is usually toward the top of the map.

Atlases can have different kinds of maps.

Isn't a map just a map?

You can make a map about anything! All you need is information.

NORTH AMERICA.

A map can help you get around. But a map can also teach you about other things.

This is a historical map. It shows North America in 1841.

The maps in a road atlas show roads. You can find out how to get places. You can go to the zoo, the airport, or another city.

Chicago

A small, close-up map of part of a large map is an inset map. Road atlases often have inset maps of cities.

Polital maps show the borders
of countries. You can see what
land belongs to each country.

Political maps can
also show states
and counties.

It looks like a patchwork quilt!

25

Thematic maps are for specific topics. A thematic map can show where wild animals live.

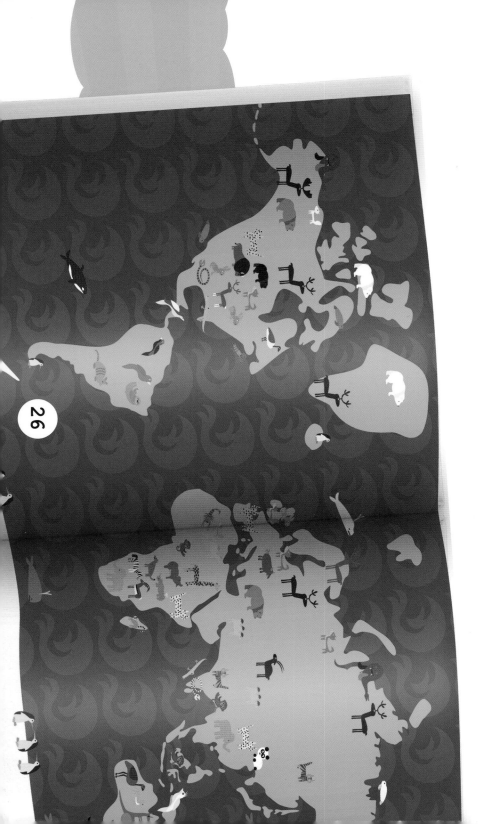

Many thematic maps use pictures to show where different things are.

Africa

N
W · E
S

A physical map shows the Earth's surface. It includes things such as mountains, lakes, rivers, and oceans.

Where is the largest lake in the world?

Are there mountains in China?

With an atlas, you can discover the world!